French Macarons Recipes

Recipes

Dessert Baking Cookbook

MARIA SOBININA

BRILLIANTkitchenideas.com

DEDICATION

This book is dedicated to my beautiful family and friends, as well as to you, my reader. I am happy to share the amazing joy of baking with you.

MARIA XOXO

TABLE OF CONTENTS

French Macarons with Buttercream Filling

INGREDIENTS:

FOR THE SHELLS:

1 Cup **Almond flour**, finely ground

1 ½ Cups **Sugar**, cane, white, powdered

1 Cup **Sugar**, cane, white, granulated

½ Cup **Blueberries**, fresh or frozen

½ and ½ teaspoons **Salt,** sea, fine

3 **Eggs**, whites

½ teaspoon Vanilla, extract, pure

FOR THE BUTTERCREAM FILLING:

8 Oz **Butter**, unsalted, softened

2 Cups **Sugar**, powdered, sifted

1 Cup **Heavy Cream**

1 teaspoon Vanilla, extract, pure

FOR THE CHOCOLATE GLAZE: (optional)

1 Cup **Chocolate**, dark, bakers

½ Cups **Sugar**, white, cane, powdered

½ Cup **Heavy Whipping Cream**

1 teaspoon **Vanilla**, pure, extract

½ teaspoon **Salt**, sea, fine

EQUIPMENT:

Small, medium and (2) large mixing bowls, Saucepan, Heatproof bowl, Baking sheet, Parchment paper, Stand mixer, equipped with the paddle attachments, Food scale or measuring cups set, Pastry piping bag, ¼ inch round piping tip, Cooling rack, Cake decorating piping tips and bags (optional).

PREPARATION:

MAKE THE MACARONS:

Step 1: Combine almond flour, powdered sugar, and ½ teaspoons of salt in a medium mixing bowl. Whisk until all is combines. Sift through a fine-mesh sieve into a large mixing bowl.

Step 2: If you use frozen blueberries, place them into a small mixing bowl and set outside to fully thaw. Mash blueberries with a fork in a small mixing bowl.

Step 3: In a bowl of a stand mixer, add egg whites and a ½ teaspoon of salt. Beat with a paddle attachment until stiff peaks start to form. Gradually add granulated sugar. Keep mixing until fully incorporated. Add mashed blueberries and vanilla extract and beat again. In the end, you will have stiff peaks that won't leak out if you turn the bowl upside down.

Step 4: Little at a time, add almond flour mixture to egg mixture and gently fold it in with a spatula until all is combined. In the end, the batter will flow but will be quite thick.

Step 5: Transfer the batter into a pastry piping bag equipped with a ¼ inch piping tip.

Step 6: Line a baking sheet with parchment paper. Pipe batter into 1-inch circles, space each circle 1 inch apart. Tap the baking sheet against a table or counter top several times to release any air bubbles. Leave on a countertop for 15-20 minutes to rise and set.

Step 7: Preheat the oven to 300°F. Place the baking sheet into the oven. Bake for 15-17 minutes, flip half time.

Transfer into a cooling rack and let macarons cool completely.

MAKE THE BUTTERCREAM FILLING:

Step 1: In a bowl of a stand mixer, add softened butter and beat it with the paddle attachment for 1-2 minutes until it becomes light and fluffy.

Step 2: Sift in the powdered sugar and continue beating until the sugar is fully incorporated. Add vanilla extract and beat again. Little by little, add heavy cream until you achieve the desired consistency.

MAKE THE CHOCOLATE GLAZE: (optional)

Step 1: Place chocolate into a heatproof bowl over a water bath. Heat over low-medium heat until the chocolate melts. Remove from heat and set aside.

Step 2: Place heavy cream into a bowl of stand mixer. Beat on medium speed with the paddle attachment until cream becomes soft and fluffy.

Step 3: Add chocolate, powdered sugar, salt, and vanilla extract. Beat on medium speed for 30-45 seconds to combine. Set aside.

ASSEMBLE THE MACARONS:

Step 1: Transfer the buttercream filling unto the piping bag.

Step 2: Add just enough of buttercream on top of the macaron shell. Cover it with another macaron shell. Place into a plate.

Repeat for all macarons until they are all filled.

DECORATE THE MACARONS: (optional)

Step 1: Place the piping tip onto a pastry bag. Add the chocolate glaze into the pastry bag. Pipe the glaze and decorate the top of each macaron with chocolate. Place into the fridge to cool for one hour.

Step 2: Use cake decorating tools to decorate the top of the macarons. You can make ¼ more buttercream and use the buttercream to decorate the tops of macarons. Place buttercream into the fridge for one hour to cool.

Step 3: Once you are ready to decorate your macarons using piping tips and bags, remove the cooled buttercream from the fridge.

Place cooled buttercream into a piping bag and start piping swirls and flowers. You can also add food coloring. *(We recommend using natural food coloring instead of artificial colors).*

Store Macarons with Buttercream Filling in the refrigerator for up to one week or up to one month in the freezer.

You may have extra filling left. You can freeze it and use it in other baking projects. The filling will keep for up to one month in the freezer. Defreeze and beat the filling with the paddle attachment before using.

FRENCH MACARONS WITH CARAMEL FILLING

INGREDIENTS:

FOR THE SHELLS:

1 Cup **Almond flour**, finely ground

1 ½ Cups **Sugar**, cane, white, powdered

1 Cup **Sugar**, cane, white, granulated

2 teaspoons **Turmeric**, powder

½ and ½ teaspoons **Salt,** sea, fine

3 **Eggs**, whites

½ teaspoon Vanilla, extract, pure

FOR THE CARAMEL FILLING:

1 cup **Sugar**, brown

1/3 cup **Milk**

2 tablespoons **Butter**, unsalted, softened

1 tablespoon **Cream**, heavy

1 teaspoon **Vanilla**, pure, extract

1/8 teaspoon **Salt**

FOR THE CHOCOLATE GLAZE: (optional)

1 Cup **Chocolate**, dark, bakers

½ Cups **Sugar**, white, cane, powdered

½ Cup **Heavy Whipping Cream**

1 teaspoon **Vanilla**, pure, extract

½ teaspoon **Salt**, sea, fine

EQUIPMENT:

Small, medium and (2) large mixing bowls, Large saucepan, Heatproof bowl, Baking sheet, Parchment paper, Stand mixer, equipped with the paddle attachments, Food scale or measuring cups set, Pastry piping bag, ¼ inch round piping tip, Cooling rack, Cake decorating piping tips and bags (optional).

PREPARATION:

MAKE THE MACARONS:

Step 1: Combine almond flour, powdered sugar, turmeric powder, and ½ teaspoons of salt in a medium mixing bowl. Whisk until all is combines. Sift through a fine-mesh sieve into a large mixing bowl.

Step 2: In a bowl of a stand mixer, add egg whites and a ½ teaspoon of salt. Beat with a paddle attachment until stiff peaks start to form. Gradually add granulated sugar. Keep mixing until fully incorporated. Add vanilla extract and beat again. In the end, you will have stiff peaks that won't leak out if you turn the bowl upside down.

Step 3: Little at a time, add almond flour mixture to egg mixture and gently fold it in with a spatula until all is combined. In the end, the batter will flow but will be quite thick.

Step 4: Transfer the batter into a pastry piping bag equipped with a ¼ inch piping tip.

Step 5: Line a baking sheet with parchment paper. Pipe batter into 1-inch circles, space each circle 1 inch apart. Tap the baking sheet against a table or counter top several times to release any air bubbles. Leave on a countertop for 15-20 minutes to rise and set.

Step 6: Preheat the oven to 300°F. Place the baking sheet into the oven. Bake for 15-17 minutes, flip half time.

Transfer into a cooling rack and let macarons cool completely.

MAKE THE CARAMEL FILLING:

Step 1: In a large saucepan, combine brown sugar, salt, butter, and milk. Cook over medium heat, stirring until the mixture comes to a boil and sugar dissolves.

Cool to lukewarm (110°F).

Step 2: Transfer the mixture into a bowl of stand mixer and beat until it begins to thicken.

Add vanilla and heavy cream and beat for another 30-45 seconds until frosting becomes smooth.

Place into the fridge to cool.

MAKE THE CHOCOLATE GLAZE: (optional)

Step 1: Place chocolate into a heatproof bowl over a water bath. Heat over low-medium heat until the chocolate melts. Remove from heat and set aside.

Step 2: Place heavy cream into a bowl of stand mixer. Beat on medium speed with the paddle attachment until cream becomes soft and fluffy.

Step 3: Add chocolate, powdered sugar, salt, and vanilla extract. Beat on medium speed for 30-45 seconds to combine. Set aside.

ASSEMBLE THE MACARONS:

Step 1: Transfer the buttercream filling unto the piping bag.

Step 2: Add just enough of buttercream on top of the macaron shell. Cover it with another macaron shell. Place into a plate.

Repeat for all macarons until they are all filled.

DECORATE THE MACARONS: (optional)

Step 1: Place the piping tip onto a pastry bag. Add the chocolate glaze into the pastry bag. Pipe the glaze and decorate the top of each macaron with chocolate. Place into the fridge to cool for one hour.

Step 2: Use cake decorating tools to decorate the top of the macarons. You can make ¼ more buttercream and use the buttercream to decorate the tops of macarons. Place buttercream into the fridge for one hour to cool.

Step 3: Once you are ready to decorate your macarons using piping tips and bags, remove the cooled buttercream from the fridge.

Place cooled buttercream into a piping bag and start piping swirls and flowers.

You can also add food coloring. *(We recommend using natural food coloring instead of artificial colors).*

Store Macarons with Caramel Filling in the refrigerator for up to one week or up to one month in the freezer.

You may have extra filling left. You can freeze it and use it in other baking projects. The filling will keep for up to one month in the freezer. Defreeze and beat the filling with the paddle attachment before using.

CHOCOLATE MACARONS WITH HAZELNUT FILLING

INGREDIENTS:

FOR THE SHELLS:

1 Cup **Almond flour**, finely ground

1 ½ Cups **Sugar**, cane, white, powdered

1 Cup **Sugar**, cane, white, granulated

½ Cup **Cocoa**, powder, unsweetened

½ and ½ teaspoons **Salt,** sea, fine

3 **Eggs**, whites

½ teaspoon Vanilla, extract, pure

FOR THE HAZELNUT FILLING:

8 Oz **Cream cheese**, softened

4 Oz cup **Butter**, unsalted, softened

1 cup **Chocolate-hazelnut**, spread

1 tablespoon **Milk**

FOR THE CHOCOLATE GLAZE: (optional)

1 Cup **Chocolate**, dark, bakers

½ Cups **Sugar**, white, cane, powdered

½ Cup **Heavy Whipping Cream**

1 teaspoon **Vanilla**, pure, extract

½ teaspoon **Salt**, sea, fine

EQUIPMENT:

Small, medium and (2) large mixing bowls, Saucepan, Heatproof bowl, Baking sheet, Parchment paper, Stand mixer, equipped with the paddle attachments, Food scale or measuring cups set, Pastry piping bag, ¼ inch round piping tip, Cooling rack, Cake decorating piping tips and bags (optional).

PREPARATION:

MAKE THE MACARONS:

Step 1: Combine almond flour, powdered sugar, cocoa powder, and ½ teaspoons of salt in a medium mixing bowl. Whisk until all is combines. Sift through a fine-mesh sieve into a large mixing bowl.

Step 2: In a bowl of a stand mixer, add egg whites and a ½ teaspoon of salt. Beat with a paddle attachment until stiff peaks start to form. Gradually add granulated sugar. Keep mixing until fully incorporated. Add vanilla extract and beat again. In the end, you will have stiff peaks that won't leak out if you turn the bowl upside down.

Step 3: Little at a time, add almond flour mixture to egg mixture and gently fold it in with a spatula until all is combined. In the end, the batter will flow but will be quite thick.

Step 4: Transfer the batter into a pastry piping bag equipped with a ¼ inch piping tip.

Step 5: Line a baking sheet with parchment paper. Pipe batter into 1-inch circles, space each circle 1 inch apart. Tap the baking sheet against a table or counter top several times to release any air bubbles. Leave on a countertop for 15-20 minutes to rise and set.

Step 6: Preheat the oven to 300°F. Place the baking sheet into the oven. Bake for 15-17 minutes, flip half time.

Transfer into a cooling rack and let macarons cool completely.

MAKE THE HAZELNUT FILLING:

Step 1: Place butter and cream cheese on a kitchen countertop and leave it until it reaches room temperature.

Step 2: In a bowl of stand mixer, fitted with the paddle attachment, beat cream cheese on medium speed, for 4-5 minutes until it becomes soft and fluffy.

Step 3: Little by little add softened butter and beat on medium speed until all is incorporated and fluffy.

Step 4: Add hazelnut spread and milk and continue beating until smooth and fluffy.

Place into the fridge to cool.

MAKE THE CHOCOLATE GLAZE: (optional)

Step 1: Place chocolate into a heatproof bowl over a water bath. Heat over low-medium heat until the chocolate melts. Remove from heat and set aside.

Step 2: Place heavy cream into a bowl of stand mixer. Beat on medium speed with the paddle attachment until cream becomes soft and fluffy.

Step 3: Add chocolate, powdered sugar, salt, and vanilla extract. Beat on medium speed for 30-45 seconds to combine. Set aside.

ASSEMBLE THE MACARONS:

Step 1: Transfer the buttercream filling unto the piping bag.

Step 2: Add just enough of buttercream on top of the macaron shell. Cover it with another macaron shell. Place into a plate.

Repeat for all macarons until they are all filled.

DECORATE THE MACARONS: (optional)

Step 1: Place the piping tip onto a pastry bag. Add the chocolate glaze into the pastry bag. Pipe the glaze and decorate the top of each macaron with chocolate. Place into the fridge to cool for one hour.

Step 2: Use cake decorating tools to decorate the top of the macarons. You can make ¼ more of hazelnut buttercream and use the buttercream to decorate the tops of macarons. Place buttercream into the fridge for one hour to cool.

Step 3: Once you are ready to decorate your macarons using piping tips and bags, remove the cooled buttercream from the fridge.

Place cooled buttercream into a piping bag and start piping swirls and flowers. You can also add food coloring. *(We recommend using natural food coloring instead of artificial colors).*

Store Macarons with Hazelnut Filling in the refrigerator for up to one week or up to one month in the freezer.

You may have extra filling left. You can freeze it and use it in other baking projects. The filling will keep for up to one month in the freezer. Defreeze and beat the filling with the paddle attachment before using.

Chocolate Macarons with Date Filling

INGREDIENTS:

FOR THE SHELLS:

1 Cup **Almond flour**, finely ground

1 ½ Cups **Sugar**, cane, white, powdered

1 Cup **Sugar**, cane, white, granulated

½ Cup **Cocoa**, powder, unsweetened

½ and ½ teaspoons **Salt,** sea, fine

3 **Eggs**, whites

½ teaspoon Vanilla, extract, pure

FOR THE DATE FILLING:

1 Cup **Dates**, pitted

½ Cup **Dates**, powder (optional, or use 1 ½ Cups of Dates)

3 Oz **Butter**, unsalted, softened

5 Oz **Farmer Cheese**

½ Cups **Sugar**, white, cane, powdered

½ Cups **Sugar**, coconut, powdered (optional, use 1 cup of cane sure if not using coconut sugar)

1 teaspoon **Vanilla**, extract, pure

FOR THE CHOCOLATE GLAZE: (optional)

1 Cup **Chocolate**, dark, bakers

½ Cups **Sugar**, white, cane, powdered

½ Cup **Heavy Whipping Cream**

1 teaspoon **Vanilla**, pure, extract

½ teaspoon **Salt**, sea, fine

EQUIPMENT:

Small, medium and (2) large mixing bowls, Saucepan, Heatproof bowl, Baking sheet, Parchment paper, Stand mixer, equipped with the paddle attachments, Food scale or measuring cups set, Pastry piping bag, ¼ inch round piping tip, Cooling rack, Cake decorating piping tips and bags (optional).

PREPARATION:

MAKE THE MACARONS:

Step 1: Combine almond flour, powdered sugar, cocoa powder, and ½ teaspoons of salt in a medium mixing bowl. Whisk until all is combines. Sift through a fine-mesh sieve into a large mixing bowl.

Step 2: In a bowl of a stand mixer, add egg whites and a ½ teaspoon of salt. Beat with a paddle attachment until stiff peaks start to form. Gradually add granulated sugar. Keep mixing until fully incorporated. Add vanilla extract and beat again. In the end, you will have stiff peaks that won't leak out if you turn the bowl upside down.

Step 3: Little at a time, add almond flour mixture to egg mixture and gently fold it in with a spatula until all is combined. In the end, the batter will flow but will be quite thick.

Step 4: Transfer the batter into a pastry piping bag equipped with a ¼ inch piping tip.

Step 5: Line a baking sheet with parchment paper. Pipe batter into 1-inch circles, space each circle 1 inch apart. Tap the baking sheet against a table or counter top several times to release any air bubbles.

Leave on a countertop for 15-20 minutes to rise and set.

Step 6: Preheat the oven to 300°F. Place the baking sheet into the oven. Bake for 15-17 minutes, flip half time.

Transfer into a cooling rack and let macarons cool completely.

MAKE THE DATE FILLING:

Step 1: Place pitted dates into a small mixing bowl, cover with water and set aside to soften.

Once the dates soften, place the dates into a food processor and process until smooth. Set the bowl with date paste aside.

Step 2: Combine butter, coconut sugar, powdered dates, and powdered sugar in a bowl of stand mixer fitted with the paddle attachment (you can use a bowl and a hand mixer).

Beat on medium speed for 2 to 3 minutes until it is fully incorporated and becomes fluffy and light in color.

Step 3: Spoon by spoon, add farmers cheese and vanilla extract and beat on medium speed for 2 to 3 minutes until it is fully incorporated and becomes light and fluffy.

Step 4: Add dates paste and beat again for about 30 seconds. Make sure the filing stays thick, but smooth enough for piping into the eclairs.

Make sure the filing stays thick, but smooth enough for piping into the eclairs. If the filling is too liquid add more powdered sugar. If the filling is too thick add a bit of heavy cream. Beat for 15-30 seconds.

MAKE THE CHOCOLATE GLAZE: (optional)

Step 1: Place chocolate into a heatproof bowl over a water bath. Heat over low-medium heat until the chocolate melts. Remove from heat and set aside.

Step 2: Place heavy cream into a bowl of stand mixer. Beat on medium speed with the paddle attachment until cream becomes soft and fluffy.

Step 3: Add chocolate, powdered sugar, salt, and vanilla extract. Beat on medium speed for 30-45 seconds to combine. Set aside.

ASSEMBLE THE MACARONS:

Step 1: Transfer the buttercream filling unto the piping bag.

Step 2: Add just enough of buttercream on top of the macaron shell. Cover it with another macaron shell. Place into a plate.

Repeat for all macarons until they are all filled.

DECORATE THE MACARONS: (optional)

Step 1: Place the piping tip onto a pastry bag. Add the chocolate glaze into the pastry bag. Pipe the glaze and decorate the top of each macaron with chocolate. Place into the fridge to cool for one hour.

Step 2: Use cake decorating tools to decorate the top of the macarons. You can make ¼ more of date buttercream and use the buttercream to decorate the tops of macarons. Place buttercream into the fridge for one hour to cool.

Step 3: Once you are ready to decorate your macarons using piping tips and bags, remove the cooled buttercream from the fridge.

Place cooled buttercream into a piping bag and start piping swirls and flowers. You can also add food coloring. *(We recommend using natural food coloring instead of artificial colors).*

Store Macarons with Date Filling in the refrigerator for up to one week or up to one month in the freezer.

You may have extra filling left. You can freeze it and use it in other baking projects. The filling will keep for up to one month in the freezer. Defreeze and beat the filling with the paddle attachment before using.

Blue Magik Macarons with Plum Filling
INGREDIENTS:
FOR THE SHELLS:

1 Cup **Almond flour**, finely ground

1 ½ Cups **Sugar**, cane, white, powdered

1 Cup **Sugar**, cane, white, granulated

3 Tablespoons **Spirulina**, powder, Blue Majik

½ and ½ teaspoons **Salt,** sea, fine

3 **Eggs**, whites

½ teaspoon Vanilla, extract, pure

FOR THE PLUM FILLING:

1 ½ Cup **Plums**, dried, pitted

3 Oz **Butter**, unsalted, softened

5 Oz **Farmer Cheese**

1 Cup **Sugar**, coconut or white, cane, powdered

1 teaspoon **Vanilla**, extract, pure

FOR THE CHOCOLATE GLAZE: (optional)

1 Cup **Chocolate**, dark, bakers

½ Cups **Sugar**, white, cane, powdered

½ Cup **Heavy Whipping Cream**

1 teaspoon **Vanilla**, pure, extract

½ teaspoon **Salt**, sea, fine

EQUIPMENT:

Small, medium and (2) large mixing bowls, Saucepan, Heatproof bowl, Baking sheet, Parchment paper, Stand mixer, equipped with the paddle attachments, Food scale or measuring cups set, Pastry piping bag, ¼ inch round piping tip, Cooling rack, Cake decorating piping tips and bags (optional).

PREPARATION:

MAKE THE MACARONS:

Step 1: Combine almond flour, powdered sugar, Blue Majik spirulina powder, and ½ teaspoons of salt in a medium mixing bowl. Whisk until all is combines. Sift through a fine-mesh sieve into a large mixing bowl.

Step 2: In a bowl of a stand mixer, add egg whites and a ½ teaspoon of salt. Beat with a paddle attachment until stiff peaks start to form. Gradually add granulated sugar. Keep mixing until fully incorporated. Add vanilla extract and beat again. In the end, you will have stiff peaks that won't leak out if you turn the bowl upside down.

Step 3: Little at a time, add almond flour mixture to egg mixture and gently fold it in with a spatula until all is combined. In the end, the batter will flow but will be quite thick.

Step 4: Transfer the batter into a pastry piping bag equipped with a ¼ inch piping tip.

Step 5: Line a baking sheet with parchment paper. Pipe batter into 1-inch circles, space each circle 1 inch apart. Tap the baking sheet against a table or counter top several times to release any air bubbles. Leave on a countertop for 15-20 minutes to rise and set.

Step 6: Preheat the oven to 300˚F. Place the baking sheet into the oven. Bake for 15-17 minutes, flip half time.

Transfer into a cooling rack and let macarons cool completely.

MAKE THE PLUM FILLING:

Step 1: Place pitted plums into a small mixing bowl, cover with water and set aside for about an hour (or as much as overnight) to soften.

Once the plums soften, place the plums into a food processor and process until smooth. Set the bowl with plum paste aside.

Step 2: Combine butter and coconut sugar in a bowl of stand mixer fitted with the paddle attachment (you can use a bowl and a hand mixer).

Beat on medium speed for 2 to 3 minutes until it is fully incorporated and becomes fluffy and light in color.

Step 3: Spoon by spoon, add farmers cheese and vanilla extract and beat on medium speed for 2 to 3 minutes until it is fully incorporated and becomes light and fluffy.

Step 4: Little by little add plum paste and beat again for about 30 seconds.

Make sure the filing stays thick, but smooth enough for piping into the eclairs. If the filling is too liquid add more powdered sugar. If the filling is too thick add a bit of heavy cream. Beat for 15-30 seconds.

MAKE THE CHOCOLATE GLAZE: (optional)

Step 1: Place chocolate into a heatproof bowl over a water bath. Heat over low-medium heat until the chocolate melts. Remove from heat and set aside.

Step 2: Place heavy cream into a bowl of stand mixer. Beat on medium speed with the paddle attachment until cream becomes soft and fluffy.

Step 3: Add chocolate, powdered sugar, salt, and vanilla extract. Beat on medium speed for 30-45 seconds to combine. Set aside.

ASSEMBLE THE MACARONS:

Step 1: Transfer the buttercream filling unto the piping bag.

Step 2: Add just enough of buttercream on top of the macaron shell. Cover it with another macaron shell. Place into a plate.

Repeat for all macarons until they are all filled.

DECORATE THE MACARONS: (optional)

Step 1: Place the piping tip onto a pastry bag. Add the chocolate glaze into the pastry bag. Pipe the glaze and decorate the top of each macaron with chocolate. Place into the fridge to cool for one hour.

Step 2: Use cake decorating tools to decorate the top of the macarons. You can make ¼ more buttercream and use the buttercream to decorate the tops of macarons. Place buttercream into the fridge for one hour to cool.

Step 3: Once you are ready to decorate your macarons using piping tips and bags, remove the cooled buttercream from the fridge.

Place cooled buttercream into a piping bag and start piping swirls and flowers. You can also add food coloring. (*We recommend using natural food coloring instead of artificial colors*).

Store Macarons with Date Filling in the refrigerator for up to one week or up to one month in the freezer.

You may have extra filling left. You can freeze it and use it in other baking projects. The filling will keep for up to one month in the freezer. Defreeze and beat the filling with the paddle attachment before using.

FRENCH MACARONS WITH RASPBERRY FILLING

INGREDIENTS:

FOR THE SHELLS:

1 Cup **Almond flour**, finely ground

1 ½ Cups **Sugar**, cane, white, powdered

1 Cup **Sugar**, cane, white, granulated

½ Cup **Dragon fruit**, powder

½ and ½ teaspoons **Salt,** sea, fine

3 **Eggs**, whites

½ teaspoon Vanilla, extract, pure

FOR THE RASPBERRY SYRUP:

2 Cups **Raspberries**, fresh or frozen

¾ Cup **Sugar**, white, cane, granulated

1 teaspoon **Vanilla**, extract, pure

FOR THE FILLING:

2 Oz **Butter**, unsalted, softened

6 Oz **Cream Cheese**

1 Cup **Sugar**, powdered

1 teaspoon **Vanilla**, extract, pure

FOR THE CHOCOLATE GLAZE: (optional)

1 Cup **Chocolate**, dark, bakers

½ Cups **Sugar**, white, cane, powdered

½ Cup **Heavy Whipping Cream**

1 teaspoon **Vanilla**, pure, extract

½ teaspoon **Salt**, sea, fine

EQUIPMENT:

Small, medium and (2) large mixing bowls, Saucepan, Heatproof bowl, Baking sheet, Parchment paper, Stand mixer, equipped with the paddle attachments, Food scale or measuring cups set, Pastry piping bag, ¼ inch round piping tip, Cooling rack, Cake decorating piping tips and bags (optional).

PREPARATION:

MAKE THE MACARONS:

Step 1: Combine almond flour, powdered sugar, dragon fruit powder, and ½ teaspoons of salt in a medium mixing bowl. Whisk until all is combines. Sift through a fine-mesh sieve into a large mixing bowl.

Step 2: In a bowl of a stand mixer, add egg whites and a ½ teaspoon of salt. Beat with a paddle attachment until stiff peaks start to form. Gradually add granulated sugar. Keep mixing until fully incorporated. Add and vanilla extract and beat again. In the end, you will have stiff peaks that won't leak out if you turn the bowl upside down.

Step 3: Little at a time, add almond flour mixture to egg mixture and gently fold it in with a spatula until all is combined. In the end, the batter will flow but will be quite thick.

Step 4: Transfer the batter into a pastry piping bag equipped with a ¼ inch piping tip.

Step 5: Line a baking sheet with parchment paper. Pipe batter into 1-inch circles, space each circle 1 inch apart. Tap the baking sheet against a table or counter top several times to release any air bubbles. Leave on a countertop for 15-20 minutes to rise and set.

Step 6: Preheat the oven to 300°F. Place the baking sheet into the oven. Bake for 15-17 minutes, flip half time.

Transfer into a cooling rack and let macarons cool completely.

MAKE THE RASPBERRY SYRUP:

In a saucepan combine raspberries and sugar.
Mash the raspberries with a masher. Let the mixture boil over medium heat, constantly stirring it. Add vanilla extract.

Once the mixture thickens, turn off the heat and set the syrup aside to cool.

MAKE THE RASPBERRY FILLING:

Step 1: Add cream cheese into a bowl of a stand mixer fitted with the paddle attachment. Beat on medium speed for 2-3 minutes until cream cheese becomes light and fluffy.

Step 2: Little at a time add powdered sugar and softened butter. Add vanilla extract. Continue beating on medium speed until all is combined and the mixture becomes light and fluffy.

Step 3: Add 2/3 of cooled raspberries syrup and beat again for about 30 seconds. (reserve the rest of the syrup for chocolate glaze. If you are not making the glaze you can use the leftover syrup in your other baking projects).

Make sure the filing stays thick. If the filling is too liquid add more powdered sugar. Place into the fridge to cool.

MAKE THE CHOCOLATE GLAZE: (optional)

Step 1: Place chocolate into a heatproof bowl over a water bath. Heat over low-medium heat until the chocolate melts. Remove from heat and set aside.

Step 2: Place heavy cream into a bowl of stand mixer. Beat on medium speed with the paddle attachment until cream becomes soft and fluffy.

Step 3: Add chocolate, powdered sugar, salt, and vanilla extract. Beat on medium speed for 30-45 seconds to combine.

Step 4: Add the remaining cooled raspberries syrup and beat for another 30 seconds. Set aside.

ASSEMBLE THE MACARONS:

Step 1: Transfer the buttercream filling unto the piping bag.

Step 2: Add just enough of buttercream on top of the macaron shell. Cover it with another macaron shell. Place into a plate.

Repeat for all macarons until they are all filled.

DECORATE THE MACARONS: (optional)

Step 1: Place the piping tip onto a pastry bag. Add the chocolate glaze into the pastry bag. Pipe the glaze and decorate the top of each macaron with chocolate. Place into the fridge to cool for one hour.

Step 2: Use cake decorating tools to decorate the top of the macarons. You can make ¼ more buttercream and use the buttercream to decorate the tops of macarons. Place buttercream into the fridge for one hour to cool.

Step 3: Once you are ready to decorate your macarons using piping tips and bags, remove the cooled buttercream from the fridge.

Place cooled buttercream into a piping bag and start piping swirls and flowers. You can also add food coloring. *(We recommend using natural food coloring instead of artificial colors).*

Store Macarons with Raspberry Filling in the refrigerator for up to one week or up to one month in the freezer.

You may have extra filling left. You can freeze it and use it in other baking projects. The filling will keep for up to one month in the freezer. Defreeze and beat the filling with the paddle attachment before using.

FRENCH MACARONS WITH KEY LIME FILLING

INGREDIENTS:

FOR THE SHELLS:

1 Cup **Almond flour**, finely ground

1 ½ Cups **Sugar**, cane, white, powdered

1 Cup **Sugar**, cane, white, granulated

½ Cup **Green tea**, powder

½ and ½ teaspoons **Salt,** sea, fine

3 **Eggs**, whites

½ teaspoon Vanilla, extract, pure

FOR THE KEY LIME FILLING:

4 Oz **Butter**, unsalted, softened

6 Oz **Cream Cheese**

1 ½ Cup **Sugar**, powdered

1 **Lime**, juice of

1 teaspoon **Vanilla**, extract, pure

FOR THE CHOCOLATE GLAZE: (optional)

1 Cup **Chocolate**, dark, bakers

½ Cups **Sugar**, white, cane, powdered

½ Cup **Heavy Whipping Cream**

1 teaspoon **Vanilla**, pure, extract

½ teaspoon **Salt**, sea, fine

EQUIPMENT:

Small, medium and (2) large mixing bowls, Saucepan, Heatproof bowl, Baking sheet, Parchment paper, Stand mixer, equipped with the paddle attachments, Food scale or measuring cups set, Pastry piping bag, ¼ inch round piping tip, Cooling rack, Cake decorating piping tips and bags (optional).

PREPARATION:

MAKE THE MACARONS:

Step 1: Combine almond flour, powdered sugar, green tea powder, and ½ teaspoons of salt in a medium mixing bowl. Whisk until all is combines. Sift through a fine-mesh sieve into a large mixing bowl.

Step 2: In a bowl of a stand mixer, add egg whites and a ½ teaspoon of salt. Beat with a paddle attachment until stiff peaks start to form. Gradually add granulated sugar. Keep mixing until fully incorporated. Add vanilla extract and beat again. In the end, you will have stiff peaks that won't leak out if you turn the bowl upside down.

Step 3: Little at a time, add almond flour mixture to egg mixture and gently fold it in with a spatula until all is combined. In the end, the batter will flow but will be quite thick.

Step 4: Transfer the batter into a pastry piping bag equipped with a ¼ inch piping tip.

Step 5: Line a baking sheet with parchment paper. Pipe batter into 1-inch circles, space each circle 1 inch apart. Tap the baking sheet against a table or counter top several times to release any air bubbles. Leave on a countertop for 15-20 minutes to rise and set.

Step 6: Preheat the oven to 300°F. Place the baking sheet into the oven. Bake for 15-17 minutes, flip half time.

Transfer into a cooling rack and let macarons cool completely.

MAKE THE KEY LIME FILLING:

Step 1: Add cream cheese into a bowl of a stand mixer fitted with the paddle attachment. Beat on medium speed for 2-3 minutes until cream cheese becomes light and fluffy.

Step 2: Little at a time add powdered sugar and softened butter.

Add vanilla extract and lime juice. Continue beating on medium speed until all is combined and the mixture becomes light and fluffy.

Make sure the filing stays thick. If the filling is too liquid add more powdered sugar. If the filling is too thick add a bit of heavy cream. Beat for 15-30 seconds.
Place into the fridge to cool.

MAKE THE CHOCOLATE GLAZE: (optional)

Step 1: Place chocolate into a heatproof bowl over a water bath. Heat over low-medium heat until the chocolate melts. Remove from heat and set aside.

Step 2: Place heavy cream into a bowl of stand mixer. Beat on medium speed with the paddle attachment until cream becomes soft and fluffy.

Step 3: Add chocolate, powdered sugar, salt, and vanilla extract. Beat on medium speed for 30-45 seconds to combine. Set aside.

ASSEMBLE THE MACARONS:

Step 1: Transfer the buttercream filling unto the piping bag.

Step 2: Add just enough of buttercream on top of the macaron shell. Cover it with another macaron shell. Place into a plate.

Repeat for all macarons until they are all filled.

DECORATE THE MACARONS: (optional)

Step 1: Place the piping tip onto a pastry bag. Add the chocolate glaze into the pastry bag. Pipe the glaze and decorate the top of each macaron with chocolate. Place into the fridge to cool for one hour.

Step 2: Use cake decorating tools to decorate the top of the macarons. You can make ¼ more buttercream and use the buttercream to decorate the tops of macarons. Place buttercream into the fridge for one hour to cool.

Step 3: Once you are ready to decorate your macarons using piping tips and bags, remove the cooled buttercream from the fridge.

Place cooled buttercream into a piping bag and start piping swirls and flowers. You can also add food coloring. *(We recommend using natural food coloring instead of artificial colors).*

Store Macarons with Key Lime Filling in the refrigerator for up to one week or up to one month in the freezer.

You may have extra filling left. You can freeze it and use it in other baking projects. The filling will keep for up to one month in the freezer. Defreeze and beat the filling with the paddle attachment before using.

CHOCOLATE MACARONS WITH MACADAMIA NUT FILLING

INGREDIENTS:

FOR THE SHELLS:

1 Cup **Almond flour**, finely ground

1 ½ Cups **Sugar**, cane, white, powdered

1 Cup **Sugar**, cane, white, granulated

½ Cup **Cocoa**, powder, unsweetened

½ and ½ teaspoons **Salt,** sea, fine

3 **Eggs**, whites

½ teaspoon Vanilla, extract, pure

FOR THE MACADAMIA NUTS PASTE:

3 Oz **Macadamia Nuts**, raw

¼ **Lemon,** juice of

FOR THE FILLING:

2 Oz **Butter**, unsalted, softened

4 Oz **Farmers Cheese**

½ Cup **Sugar**, powdered

1 teaspoon **Vanilla**, extract, pure

FOR THE CHOCOLATE GLAZE: (optional)

1 Cup **Chocolate**, dark, bakers

½ Cups **Sugar**, white, cane, powdered

½ Cup **Heavy Whipping Cream**

1 teaspoon **Vanilla**, pure, extract

½ teaspoon **Salt**, sea, fine

EQUIPMENT:

Small, medium and (2) large mixing bowls, Saucepan, Heatproof bowl, Baking sheet, Parchment paper, Stand mixer, equipped with the paddle attachments, Food scale or measuring cups set, Pastry piping bag, ¼ inch round piping tip, Cooling rack, Cake decorating piping tips and bags (optional).

PREPARATION:

MAKE THE MACARONS:

Step 1: Combine almond flour, powdered sugar, cocoa powder, and ½ teaspoons of salt in a medium mixing bowl. Whisk until all is combines. Sift through a fine-mesh sieve into a large mixing bowl.

Step 2: In a bowl of a stand mixer, add egg whites and a ½ teaspoon of salt. Beat with a paddle attachment until stiff peaks start to form. Gradually add granulated sugar. Keep mixing until fully incorporated. Add vanilla extract and beat again. In the end, you will have stiff peaks that won't leak out if you turn the bowl upside down.

Step 3: Little at a time, add almond flour mixture to egg mixture and gently fold it in with a spatula until all is combined. In the end, the batter will flow but will be quite thick.

Step 4: Transfer the batter into a pastry piping bag equipped with a ¼ inch piping tip.

Step 5: Line a baking sheet with parchment paper. Pipe batter into 1-inch circles, space each circle 1 inch apart. Tap the baking sheet against a table or counter top several times to release any air bubbles. Leave on a countertop for 15-20 minutes to rise and set.

Step 6: Preheat the oven to 300°F. Place the baking sheet into the oven. Bake for 15-17 minutes, flip half time.

Transfer into a cooling rack and let macarons cool completely.

MAKE THE MACADAMIA NUTS PASTE:

In a food processor combine macadamia nuts with lemon juice and start processing. If the mixture becomes dry, little by little add water until the mixture becomes a smooth and thick paste. Set aside.

MAKE THE MACADAMIA NUT FILLING:

Step 1: Add farmers cheese into a bowl of a stand mixer fitted with the paddle attachment. Beat on medium speed for 2-3 minutes until farmers cheese becomes light and fluffy.

Step 2: Little at a time add powdered sugar and softened butter, continue beating on medium speed. Little by little add macadamia nuts paste. Add vanilla extract. Continue beating on medium speed until all is combined and the mixture becomes light and fluffy.

Make sure the filing stays thick. If the filling is too liquid add more powdered sugar. If the filling is too thick add a bit of heavy cream. Beat for 15-30 seconds.
Place into the fridge to cool.

MAKE THE CHOCOLATE GLAZE: (optional)

Step 1: Place chocolate into a heatproof bowl over a water bath. Heat over low-medium heat until the chocolate melts. Remove from heat and set aside.

Step 2: Place heavy cream into a bowl of stand mixer. Beat on medium speed with the paddle attachment until cream becomes soft and fluffy.

Step 3: Add chocolate, powdered sugar, salt, and vanilla extract. Beat on medium speed for 30-45 seconds to combine. Set aside.

ASSEMBLE THE MACARONS:

Step 1: Transfer the buttercream filling unto the piping bag.

Step 2: Add just enough of buttercream on top of the macaron shell. Cover it with another macaron shell. Place into a plate.

Repeat for all macarons until they are all filled.

DECORATE THE MACARONS: (optional)

Step 1: Place the piping tip onto a pastry bag. Add the chocolate glaze into the pastry bag. Pipe the glaze and decorate the top of each macaron with chocolate. Place into the fridge to cool for one hour.

Step 2: Use cake decorating tools to decorate the top of the macarons. You can make ¼ more of hazelnut buttercream and use the buttercream to decorate the tops of macarons. Place buttercream into the fridge for one hour to cool.

Step 3: Once you are ready to decorate your macarons using piping tips and bags, remove the cooled buttercream from the fridge.

Place cooled buttercream into a piping bag and start piping swirls and flowers. You can also add food coloring. *(We recommend using natural food coloring instead of artificial colors).*

Store Macarons with Macadamia Nut Filling in the refrigerator for up to one week or up to one month in the freezer.

You may have extra filling left. You can freeze it and use it in other baking projects. The filling will keep for up to one month in the freezer. Defreeze and beat the filling with the paddle attachment before using.

FRENCH MACARONS WITH PISTACHIO FILLING

INGREDIENTS:

FOR THE SHELLS:

1 Cup **Almond flour**, finely ground

1 ½ Cups **Sugar**, cane, white, powdered

1 Cup **Sugar**, cane, white, granulated

2 Tablespoons **Spirulina**, powder

½ and ½ teaspoons **Salt,** sea, fine

3 **Eggs**, whites

½ teaspoon Vanilla, extract, pure

FOR THE PISTACHIO PASTE:

3 Oz **Pistachios**, raw

¼ **Lemon,** juice of

FOR THE FILLING:

2 Oz **Butter**, unsalted, softened

4 Oz **Cream Cheese**

½ Cup **Sugar**, powdered

1 teaspoon **Vanilla**, extract, pure

FOR THE CHOCOLATE GLAZE: (optional)

1 Cup **Chocolate**, dark, bakers

½ Cups **Sugar**, white, cane, powdered

½ Cup **Heavy Whipping Cream**

1 teaspoon **Vanilla**, pure, extract

½ teaspoon **Salt**, sea, fine

EQUIPMENT:

Small, medium and (2) large mixing bowls, Saucepan, Heatproof bowl, Baking sheet, Parchment paper, Stand mixer, equipped with the paddle attachments, Food scale or measuring cups set, Pastry piping bag, ¼ inch round piping tip, Cooling rack, Cake decorating piping tips and bags (optional).

PREPARATION:

MAKE THE MACARONS:

Step 1: Combine almond flour, powdered sugar, spirulina powder, and ½ teaspoons of salt in a medium mixing bowl. Whisk until all is combines.

Sift through a fine-mesh sieve into a large mixing bowl.

Step 2: In a bowl of a stand mixer, add egg whites and a ½ teaspoon of salt. Beat with a paddle attachment until stiff peaks start to form. Gradually add granulated sugar. Keep mixing until fully incorporated. Add vanilla extract and beat again. In the end, you will have stiff peaks that won't leak out if you turn the bowl upside down.

Step 3: Little at a time, add almond flour mixture to egg mixture and gently fold it in with a spatula until all is combined. In the end, the batter will flow but will be quite thick.

Step 4: Transfer the batter into a pastry piping bag equipped with a ¼ inch piping tip.

Step 5: Line a baking sheet with parchment paper. Pipe batter into 1-inch circles, space each circle 1 inch apart. Tap the baking sheet against a table or counter top several times to release any air bubbles. Leave on a countertop for 15-20 minutes to rise and set.

Step 6: Preheat the oven to 300°F. Place the baking sheet into the oven. Bake for 15-17 minutes, flip half time.

Transfer into a cooling rack and let macarons cool completely.

MAKE THE PISTACHIO PASTE:

In a food processor combine pistachios with lemon juice and start processing. If the mixture becomes dry, little by little add water until the mixture becomes a smooth and thick paste. Set aside.

MAKE THE PISTACHIO FILLING:

Step 1: Add cream cheese into a bowl of a stand mixer fitted with the paddle attachment. Beat on medium speed for 2-3 minutes until cream cheese becomes light and fluffy.

Step 2: Little at a time add powdered sugar and softened butter, continue beating on medium speed. Little by little add pistachio paste. Add vanilla extract. Continue beating on medium speed until all is combined and the mixture becomes light and fluffy.

Make sure the filing stays thick, but smooth enough for piping into the eclairs. If the filling is too liquid add more powdered sugar. If the filling is too thick add a bit of heavy cream. Beat for 15-30 seconds.
Place into the fridge to cool.

MAKE THE CHOCOLATE GLAZE: (optional)

Step 1: Place chocolate into a heatproof bowl over a water bath.

Heat over low-medium heat until the chocolate melts. Remove from heat and set aside.

Step 2: Place heavy cream into a bowl of stand mixer. Beat on medium speed with the paddle attachment until cream becomes soft and fluffy.

Step 3: Add chocolate, powdered sugar, salt, and vanilla extract. Beat on medium speed for 30-45 seconds to combine. Set aside.

ASSEMBLE THE MACARONS:

Step 1: Transfer the buttercream filling unto the piping bag.

Step 2: Add just enough of buttercream on top of the macaron shell. Cover it with another macaron shell. Place into a plate.

Repeat for all macarons until they are all filled.

DECORATE THE MACARONS: (optional)

Step 1: Place the piping tip onto a pastry bag. Add the chocolate glaze into the pastry bag. Pipe the glaze and decorate the top of each macaron with chocolate. Place into the fridge to cool for one hour.

Step 2: Use cake decorating tools to decorate the top of the macarons. You can make ¼ more buttercream and use the buttercream to decorate the tops of macarons. Place buttercream into the fridge for one hour to cool.

Step 3: Once you are ready to decorate your macarons using piping tips and bags, remove the cooled buttercream from the fridge.

Place cooled buttercream into a piping bag and start piping swirls and flowers. You can also add food coloring. *(We recommend using natural food coloring instead of artificial colors).*

Store Macarons with Pistachio Filling in the refrigerator for up to one week or up to one month in the freezer.

You may have extra filling left. You can freeze it and use it in other baking projects. The filling will keep for up to one month in the freezer. Defreeze and beat the filling with the paddle attachment before using.

Chocolate Macarons with Chocolate Filling

INGREDIENTS:

FOR THE SHELLS:

1 Cup **Almond flour**, finely ground

1 ½ Cups **Sugar**, cane, white, powdered

1 Cup **Sugar**, cane, white, granulated

½ Cup **Cocoa**, powder, unsweetened

½ and ½ teaspoons **Salt,** sea, fine

3 **Eggs**, whites

½ teaspoon Vanilla, extract, pure

FOR THE CHOCOLATE FILLING:

2 Cups **Heavy Cream** or **Whipping Cream**

¼ Cup **Sugar**, white, cane, powdered

½ Cup **Cocoa,** powder, unsweetened

1 teaspoon **Vanilla**, pure, extract

FOR THE CHOCOLATE GLAZE: (optional)

1 Cup **Chocolate**, dark, bakers

½ Cups **Sugar**, white, cane, powdered

½ Cup **Heavy Whipping Cream**

1 teaspoon **Vanilla**, pure, extract

½ teaspoon **Salt**, sea, fine

EQUIPMENT:

Small, medium and (2) large mixing bowls, Saucepan, Heatproof bowl, Baking sheet, Parchment paper, Stand mixer, equipped with the paddle attachments, Food scale or measuring cups set, Pastry piping bag, ¼ inch round piping tip, Cooling rack, Cake decorating piping tips and bags (optional).

PREPARATION:

MAKE THE MACARONS:

Step 1: Combine almond flour, powdered sugar, cocoa powder, and ½ teaspoons of salt in a medium mixing bowl. Whisk until all is combines. Sift through a fine-mesh sieve into a large mixing bowl.

Step 2: In a bowl of a stand mixer, add egg whites and a ½ teaspoon of salt. Beat with a paddle attachment until stiff peaks start to form. Gradually add granulated sugar. Keep mixing until fully incorporated. Add vanilla extract and beat again. In the end, you will have stiff peaks that won't leak out if you turn the bowl upside down.

Step 3: Little at a time, add almond flour mixture to egg mixture and gently fold it in with a spatula until all is combined. In the end, the batter will flow but will be quite thick.

Step 4: Transfer the batter into a pastry piping bag equipped with a ¼ inch piping tip.

Step 5: Line a baking sheet with parchment paper. Pipe batter into 1-inch circles, space each circle 1 inch apart. Tap the baking sheet against a table or counter top several times to release any air bubbles. Leave on a countertop for 15-20 minutes to rise and set.

Step 6: Preheat the oven to 300˚F. Place the baking sheet into the oven. Bake for 15-17 minutes, flip half time.

Transfer into a cooling rack and let macarons cool completely.

MAKE THE CHOCOLATE FILLING:

Step 1: Add heavy cream into a bowl of stand mixer fitted with the whisk attachment. Start wiping on high speed.

Step 2: Little at a time add powdered sugar and cocoa powder and continue wiping on high speed. Add vanilla extract. Beat the mixture into stiff cream. Do not overbeat or the cream will crumble.

Make sure the filing stays thick. If the filling is too liquid add more powdered sugar. If the filling is too thick add a bit of heavy cream. Beat for 15-30 seconds.
Place into the fridge to cool.

MAKE THE CHOCOLATE GLAZE: (optional)

Step 1: Place chocolate into a heatproof bowl over a water bath. Heat over low-medium heat until the chocolate melts. Remove from heat and set aside.

Step 2: Place heavy cream into a bowl of stand mixer. Beat on medium speed with the paddle attachment until cream becomes soft and fluffy.

Step 3: Add chocolate, powdered sugar, salt, and vanilla extract. Beat on medium speed for 30-45 seconds to combine. Set aside.

ASSEMBLE THE MACARONS:

Step 1: Transfer the buttercream filling unto the piping bag.

Step 2: Add just enough of buttercream on top of the macaron shell. Cover it with another macaron shell. Place into a plate.

Repeat for all macarons until they are all filled.

DECORATE THE MACARONS: (optional)

Step 1: Place the piping tip onto a pastry bag. Add the chocolate glaze into the pastry bag. Pipe the glaze and decorate the top of each macaron with chocolate. Place into the fridge to cool for one hour.

Step 2: Use cake decorating tools to decorate the top of the macarons. You can make ¼ more of hazelnut buttercream and use the buttercream to decorate the tops of macarons. Place buttercream into the fridge for one hour to cool.

Step 3: Once you are ready to decorate your macarons using piping tips and bags, remove the cooled buttercream from the fridge.

Place cooled buttercream into a piping bag and start piping swirls and flowers. You can also add food coloring. *(We recommend using natural food coloring instead of artificial colors).*

Store Chocolate Macarons with Chocolate Filling in the refrigerator for up to one week or up to one month in the freezer.

You may have extra filling left. You can freeze it and use it in other baking projects. The filling will keep for up to one month in the freezer. Defreeze and beat the filling with the paddle attachment before using.

FRENCH MACARONS WITH BLUEBERRY FILLING

INGREDIENTS:

FOR THE SHELLS:

1 Cup **Almond flour**, finely ground

1 ½ Cups **Sugar**, cane, white, powdered

1 Cup **Sugar**, cane, white, granulated

½ Cup **Blueberries**, fresh or frozen

½ and ½ teaspoons **Salt,** sea, fine

3 **Eggs**, whites

½ teaspoon Vanilla, extract, pure

FOR THE BLUEBERRY SYRUP:

2 Cups **Blueberries**, fresh or frozen

¾ Cup **Sugar**, white, cane, granulated

1 teaspoon **Vanilla**, extract, pure

FOR THE FILLING:

2 Oz **Butter**, unsalted, softened

6 Oz **Farmer Cheese**

1 Cup **Sugar**, white, cane, powdered

1 teaspoon **Vanilla**, extract, pure

FOR THE CHOCOLATE GLAZE: (optional)

1 Cup **Chocolate**, dark, bakers

½ Cups **Sugar**, white, cane, powdered

½ Cup **Heavy Whipping Cream**

1 teaspoon **Vanilla**, pure, extract

½ teaspoon **Salt**, sea, fine

EQUIPMENT:

Small, medium and (2) large mixing bowls, Saucepan, Heatproof bowl, Baking sheet, Parchment paper, Stand mixer, equipped with the paddle attachments, Food scale or measuring cups set, Pastry piping bag, ¼ inch round piping tip, Cooling rack, Cake decorating piping tips and bags (optional).

PREPARATION:

MAKE THE MACARONS:

Step 1: Combine almond flour, powdered sugar, and ½ teaspoons of salt in a medium mixing bowl.

Whisk until all is combines. Sift through a fine-mesh sieve into a large mixing bowl.

Step 2: If you use frozen blueberries, place them into a small mixing bowl and set outside to fully thaw. Mash blueberries with a fork in a small mixing bowl.

Step 3: In a bowl of a stand mixer, add egg whites and a ½ teaspoon of salt. Beat with a paddle attachment until stiff peaks start to form. Gradually add granulated sugar. Keep mixing until fully incorporated. Add mashed blueberries and vanilla extract and beat again. In the end, you will have stiff peaks that won't leak out if you turn the bowl upside down.

Step 4: Little at a time, add almond flour mixture to egg mixture and gently fold it in with a spatula until all is combined. In the end, the batter will flow but will be quite thick.

Step 5: Transfer the batter into a pastry piping bag equipped with a ¼ inch piping tip.

Step 6: Line a baking sheet with parchment paper. Pipe batter into 1-inch circles, space each circle 1 inch apart. Tap the baking sheet against a table or counter top several times to release any air bubbles.

Leave on a countertop for 15-20 minutes to rise and set.

Step 7: Preheat the oven to 300°F. Place the baking sheet into the oven. Bake for 15-17 minutes, flip half time.

Transfer into a cooling rack and let macarons cool completely.

MAKE THE BLUEBERRY SYRUP:

In a small saucepan combine blueberries and sugar. Mash the blueberries with a masher. Let the mixture boil over medium heat, constantly stirring it. Add vanilla extract.

Once the mixture thickens, turn off the heat and set the syrup aside to cool.

MAKE THE FILLING:

Step 1: Combine butter and powdered sugar in a bowl of stand mixer fitted with the paddle attachment (you can use a bowl and a hand mixer).

Beat on medium speed for 2 to 3 minutes until it is fully incorporated and becomes fluffy and light in color.

Step 2: Spoon by spoon, add farmers cheese and vanilla extract and beat on medium speed for 2 to 3 minutes until it is fully incorporated and becomes light and fluffy.

Step 3: Add 2/3 of cooled blueberries syrup and beat again for about 30 seconds. (reserve the rest of the syrup for chocolate glaze. If you are not making the glaze you can use the leftover syrup in your other baking projects).

Make sure the filing stays. If the filling is too liquid add more powdered sugar. If the filling is too thick add a bit of heavy cream. Beat for 15-30 seconds.

MAKE THE CHOCOLATE GLAZE: (optional)

Step 1: Place chocolate into a heatproof bowl over a water bath. Heat over low-medium heat until the chocolate melts. Remove from heat and set aside.

Step 2: Place heavy cream into a bowl of stand mixer. Beat on medium speed with the paddle attachment until cream becomes soft and fluffy.

Step 3: Add chocolate, powdered sugar, salt, and vanilla extract. Beat on medium speed for 30-45 seconds to combine. Add the remaining cooled blueberries syrup and beat for another 30 seconds. Set aside.

ASSEMBLE THE MACARONS:

Step 1: Transfer the buttercream filling unto the piping bag.

Step 2: Add just enough of buttercream on top of the macaron shell. Cover it with another macaron shell. Place into a plate.

Repeat for all macarons until they are all filled.

DECORATE THE MACARONS: (optional)

Step 1: Place the piping tip onto a pastry bag. Add the chocolate glaze into the pastry bag. Pipe the glaze and decorate the top of each macaron with chocolate. Place into the fridge to cool for one hour.

Step 2: Use cake decorating tools to decorate the top of the macarons. You can make ¼ more buttercream and use the buttercream to decorate the tops of macarons. Place buttercream into the fridge for one hour to cool.

Step 3: Once you are ready to decorate your macarons using piping tips and bags, remove the cooled buttercream from the fridge.

Place cooled buttercream into a piping bag and start piping swirls and flowers. You can also add food coloring. *(We recommend using natural food coloring instead of artificial colors).*

Store Macarons with Blueberry Filling in the refrigerator for up to one week or up to one month in the freezer.

You may have extra filling left. You can freeze it and use it in other baking projects. The filling will keep for up to one month in the freezer. Defreeze and beat the filling with the paddle attachment before using.

Chocolate Macarons with Condensed Milk Filling

INGREDIENTS:

FOR THE SHELLS:

1 Cup **Almond flour**, finely ground

1 ½ Cups **Sugar**, cane, white, powdered

1 Cup **Sugar**, cane, white, granulated

½ Cup **Cocoa**, powder, unsweetened

½ and ½ teaspoons **Salt,** sea, fine

3 **Eggs**, whites

½ teaspoon Vanilla, extract, pure

FOR THE CONDENSED MILK FILLING:

6 Oz **Butter**, unsalted, softened

2 Cups **Milk**, condensed, sweetened

2 ½ cups **Sugar**, powdered

1 teaspoon **Vanilla**, extract, pure

FOR THE CHOCOLATE GLAZE: (optional)

1 Cup **Chocolate**, dark, bakers

½ Cups **Sugar**, white, cane, powdered

½ Cup **Heavy Whipping Cream**

1 teaspoon **Vanilla**, pure, extract

½ teaspoon **Salt**, sea, fine

EQUIPMENT:

Small, medium and (2) large mixing bowls, Saucepan, Heatproof bowl, Baking sheet, Parchment paper, Stand mixer, equipped with the paddle attachments, Food scale or measuring cups set, Pastry piping bag, ¼ inch round piping tip, Cooling rack, Cake decorating piping tips and bags (optional).

PREPARATION:

MAKE THE MACARONS:

Step 1: Combine almond flour, powdered sugar, cocoa powder, and ½ teaspoons of salt in a medium mixing bowl. Whisk until all is combines. Sift through a fine-mesh sieve into a large mixing bowl.

Step 2: In a bowl of a stand mixer, add egg whites and a ½ teaspoon of salt. Beat with a paddle attachment until stiff peaks start to form. Gradually add granulated sugar. Keep mixing until fully incorporated. Add vanilla extract and beat again. In the end, you will have stiff peaks that won't leak out if you turn the bowl upside down.

Step 3: Little at a time, add almond flour mixture to egg mixture and gently fold it in with a spatula until all is combined. In the end, the batter will flow but will be quite thick.

Step 4: Transfer the batter into a pastry piping bag equipped with a ¼ inch piping tip.

Step 5: Line a baking sheet with parchment paper. Pipe batter into 1-inch circles, space each circle 1 inch apart. Tap the baking sheet against a table or counter top several times to release any air bubbles. Leave on a countertop for 15-20 minutes to rise and set.

Step 6: Preheat the oven to 300°F. Place the baking sheet into the oven. Bake for 15-17 minutes, flip half time.

Transfer into a cooling rack and let macarons cool completely.

MAKE THE CONDENSED MILK FILLING:

Step 1: Combine butter and powdered sugar in a bowl of stand mixer fitted with the paddle attachment (you can use a bowl and a hand mixer).

Beat on medium speed for 2 to 3 minutes until it is fully incorporated and becomes fluffy and light in color.

Step 2: Spoon by spoon, add condensed milk and vanilla extract and beat on medium speed for 2 to 3 minutes until it is fully incorporated and becomes light and fluffy.

Make sure the filing stays thick. If the filling is too liquid add more powdered sugar. If the filling is too thick add a bit of heavy cream. Beat for 15-30 seconds.

Place into the fridge to cool.

MAKE THE CHOCOLATE GLAZE: (optional)

Step 1: Place chocolate into a heatproof bowl over a water bath. Heat over low-medium heat until the chocolate melts. Remove from heat and set aside.

Step 2: Place heavy cream into a bowl of stand mixer. Beat on medium speed with the paddle attachment until cream becomes soft and fluffy.

Step 3: Add chocolate, powdered sugar, salt, and vanilla extract. Beat on medium speed for 30-45 seconds to combine. Set aside.

ASSEMBLE THE MACARONS:

Step 1: Transfer the buttercream filling unto the piping bag.

Step 2: Add just enough of buttercream on top of the macaron shell. Cover it with another macaron shell. Place into a plate.

Repeat for all macarons until they are all filled.

DECORATE THE MACARONS: (optional)

Step 1: Place the piping tip onto a pastry bag. Add the chocolate glaze into the pastry bag. Pipe the glaze and decorate the top of each macaron with chocolate. Place into the fridge to cool for one hour.

Step 2: Use cake decorating tools to decorate the top of the macarons. You can make ¼ more of hazelnut buttercream and use the buttercream to decorate the tops of macarons. Place buttercream into the fridge for one hour to cool.

Step 3: Once you are ready to decorate your macarons using piping tips and bags, remove the cooled buttercream from the fridge.

Place cooled buttercream into a piping bag and start piping swirls and flowers. You can also add food coloring. *(We recommend using natural food coloring instead of artificial colors).*

Store Chocolate Macarons with Condensed Milk Filling in the refrigerator for up to one week or up to one month in the freezer.

You may have extra filling left. You can freeze it and use it in other baking projects. The filling will keep for up to one month in the freezer. Defreeze and beat the filling with the paddle attachment before using.

FRENCH MACARONS WITH ORANGE BUTTERCREAM FILLING

INGREDIENTS:

FOR THE SHELLS:

1 Cup **Almond flour**, finely ground

1 ½ Cups **Sugar**, cane, white, powdered

1 Cup **Sugar**, cane, white, granulated

½ Cup **Beet**, powder

½ and ½ teaspoons **Salt,** sea, fine

3 **Eggs**, whites

½ teaspoon Vanilla, extract, pure

FOR THE ORANGE SYRUP:

1 **Orange**, small, fresh, juice of

½ Cup **Sugar**, coconut

1 teaspoon **Vanilla**, extract, pure

FOR THE FILLING:

2 Cups **Heavy Cream** or **Whipping Cream**

¼ Cup **Sugar**, white, cane, powdered

1 teaspoon **Vanilla**, pure, extract

FOR THE CHOCOLATE GLAZE: (optional)

1 Cup **Chocolate**, dark, bakers

½ Cups **Sugar**, white, cane, powdered

½ Cup **Heavy Whipping Cream**

1 teaspoon **Vanilla**, pure, extract

½ teaspoon **Salt**, sea, fine

EQUIPMENT:

Small, medium and (2) large mixing bowls, Saucepan, Heatproof bowl, Baking sheet, Parchment paper, Stand mixer, equipped with the paddle attachments, Food scale or measuring cups set, Pastry piping bag, ¼ inch round piping tip, Cooling rack, Cake decorating piping tips and bags (optional).

PREPARATION:

MAKE THE MACARONS:

Step 1: Combine almond flour, powdered sugar, beet powder, and ½ teaspoons of salt in a medium mixing bowl. Whisk until all is combines. Sift through a fine-mesh sieve into a large mixing bowl.

Step 2: In a bowl of a stand mixer, add egg whites and a ½ teaspoon of salt. Beat with a paddle attachment until stiff peaks start to form. Gradually add granulated sugar. Keep mixing until fully incorporated. Add vanilla extract and beat again. In the end, you will have stiff peaks that won't leak out if you turn the bowl upside down.

Step 3: Little at a time, add almond flour mixture to egg mixture and gently fold it in with a spatula until all is combined. In the end, the batter will flow but will be quite thick.

Step 4: Transfer the batter into a pastry piping bag equipped with a ¼ inch piping tip.

Step 5: Line a baking sheet with parchment paper. Pipe batter into 1-inch circles, space each circle 1 inch apart. Tap the baking sheet against a table or counter top several times to release any air bubbles. Leave on a countertop for 15-20 minutes to rise and set.

Step 6: Preheat the oven to 300°F. Place the baking sheet into the oven. Bake for 15-17 minutes, flip half time.

Transfer into a cooling rack and let macarons cool completely.

MAKE THE ORANGE SYRUP:

In a small saucepan combine orange juice and coconut sugar. Let the mixture boil over medium heat, constantly stirring it. Add vanilla extract.

Once the mixture thickens, turn off the heat and set the syrup aside to cool.

MAKE THE ORANGE FILLING:

Step 1: Add heavy cream into a bowl of stand mixer fitted with the whisk attachment.
Start wiping on high speed.

Step 2: Little at a time add powdered sugar and continue wiping on high speed. Add vanilla extract. Beat the mixture into stiff cream. Do not overbeat or the cream will crumble.

Step 3: Little by little fold in cooled orange syrup. Beat again for about 30 seconds.

Make sure the filing stays thick. If the filling is too liquid add more powdered sugar. If the filling is too thick add a bit of heavy cream. Beat for 15-30 seconds.
Place into the fridge to cool.

MAKE THE CHOCOLATE GLAZE: (optional)

Step 1: Place chocolate into a heatproof bowl over a water bath.

Heat over low-medium heat until the chocolate melts. Remove from heat and set aside.

Step 2: Place heavy cream into a bowl of stand mixer. Beat on medium speed with the paddle attachment until cream becomes soft and fluffy.

Step 3: Add chocolate, powdered sugar, salt, and vanilla extract. Beat on medium speed for 30-45 seconds to combine. Set aside.

ASSEMBLE THE MACARONS:

Step 1: Transfer the buttercream filling unto the piping bag.

Step 2: Add just enough of buttercream on top of the macaron shell. Cover it with another macaron shell. Place into a plate.

Repeat for all macarons until they are all filled.

DECORATE THE MACARONS: (optional)

Step 1: Place the piping tip onto a pastry bag. Add the chocolate glaze into the pastry bag. Pipe the glaze and decorate the top of each macaron with chocolate. Place into the fridge to cool for one hour.

Step 2: Use cake decorating tools to decorate the top of the macarons.

You can make ¼ more buttercream and use the buttercream to decorate the tops of macarons. Place buttercream into the fridge for one hour to cool.

Step 3: Once you are ready to decorate your macarons using piping tips and bags, remove the cooled buttercream from the fridge.

Place cooled buttercream into a piping bag and start piping swirls and flowers. You can also add food coloring. *(We recommend using natural food coloring instead of artificial colors).*

Store Macarons with Orange Buttercream Filling in the refrigerator for up to one week or up to one month in the freezer.

You may have extra filling left. You can freeze it and use it in other baking projects. The filling will keep for up to one month in the freezer. Defreeze and beat the filling with the paddle attachment before using.

Thank You for Purchasing This Book!

I create and test recipes for you. I hope you enjoyed these recipes.

Your review of this book helps me succeed & grow. If you enjoyed this book, please leave me a short (1-2 sentence) review on Amazon.

Thank you so much for reviewing this book!

Do you have any questions?
Email me at: **Maria@BRILLIANTkithenideas.com**

MARIA SOBININA
BRILLIANT kitchen ideas

Would you like to learn cooking techniques and tips? Visit us at:

www. BRILLIANTkitchenideas.com

CPSIA information can be obtained
at www.ICGtesting.com
Printed in the USA
FSHW011248311220
77308FS

9 781095 467657